A QUARTO BOOK
First published in
Great Britain by
B. T. Batsford Ltd.
4 Fitzhardinge Street
London W1H 0AH

ISBN 0-7134-7421-1

A catalogue record
for this book is
available from the
British Library.

This book was
designed and
produced by Quarto
Publishing plc
The Old Brewery
6 Blundell Street
London N7 9BH

While every care
has been taken with
the printing of the
colour charts, the
publishers cannot
guarantee total
accuracy in every case.

CONTENTS

Blue slate

Violet

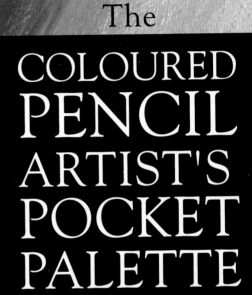

The
COLOURED
PENCIL
ARTIST'S
POCKET
PALETTE

Instant, practical visual guidance on
mixing and matching coloured
pencils to suit all subjects

Jane Strother

B.T. Batsford Ltd • London

THE COLOURS

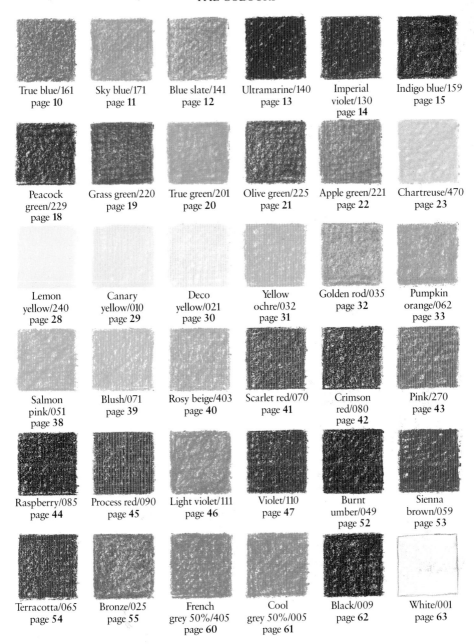

True blue/161 page 10	Sky blue/171 page 11	Blue slate/141 page 12	Ultramarine/140 page 13	Imperial violet/130 page 14	Indigo blue/159 page 15
Peacock green/229 page 18	Grass green/220 page 19	True green/201 page 20	Olive green/225 page 21	Apple green/221 page 22	Chartreuse/470 page 23
Lemon yellow/240 page 28	Canary yellow/010 page 29	Deco yellow/021 page 30	Yellow ochre/032 page 31	Golden rod/035 page 32	Pumpkin orange/062 page 33
Salmon pink/051 page 38	Blush/071 page 39	Rosy beige/403 page 40	Scarlet red/070 page 41	Crimson red/080 page 42	Pink/270 page 43
Raspberry/085 page 44	Process red/090 page 45	Light violet/111 page 46	Violet/110 page 47	Burnt umber/049 page 52	Sienna brown/059 page 53
Terracotta/065 page 54	Bronze/025 page 55	French grey 50%/405 page 60	Cool grey 50%/005 page 61	Black/009 page 62	White/001 page 63

USING THIS BOOK

Coloured pencils cannot be premixed as paints can, but rich and varied colour effects can be built up by mixing on the working surface. The purpose of this book is to provide the coloured pencil artist with an easy guide to over 800 colour overlays, using both "dry" pencils and the watersoluble variety, which can create very painterly effects.

From the vast range of coloured pencils available, we have chosen a selection of 36, and the charts show how this relatively small basic palette can be extended by mixing. The page by page chart layout provides instant visual information so that you can see at a glance how to achieve the mix you want. You may also discover some surprising new mixes and intriguing colour contrasts.

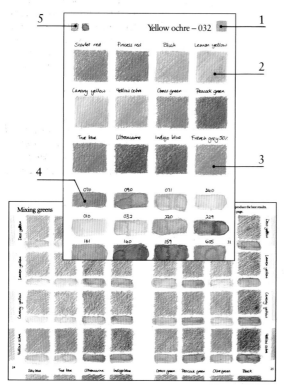

◀*Each page features one of the 36 colours, referred to as the "main" colour (1). For a visual guide to these see page 3. On each page, the main colour is laid over 12 constant "basic palette" colours (2, and see opposite), which appear in the same order every time. The main colour is also shown at the top of each page. Both "dry" and watersoluble pencils have been used for the charts. The former are referred to by name (3) and the latter by number (4). The symbols (5) denote various characteristics of the main colour.*

◀*Special features focus on secondary colours (green, orange and purple), and provide useful mixes for browns. Such colours can, of course, be bought ready made, but it can be interesting to make your own.*

THE BASIC PALETTE

The palette of 12 colours shown below provides a balanced range from across the spectrum. However, this is oney a starting point, and you may wish to add or substitute certain colours to alter the balance. For example, apple green, which is yellowish, might replace grass green, which has a blue bias.

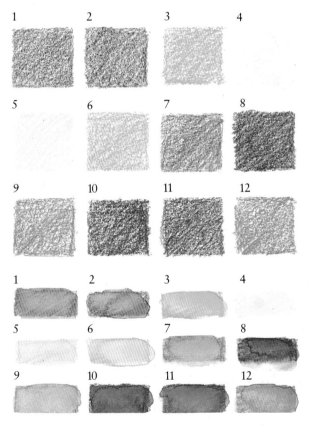

◀ *This is the basic palette used throughout the book, shown here without the addition of the main colour. In the charts (see opposite), the basic palette colours are put down first and the main colours laid on top. The colour mix varies according to which colour is laid first. It is also much affected by the pressure of the pencil, and the charts have been graded light to dark to show something of these effects.*

The names refer to the Berol dry pencils and the numbers in brackets to the Caran d'Ache watersoluble pencils.

1 *Scarlet red (070)*
2 *Process red (090)*
3 *Blush (071)*
4 *Lemon yellow (240)*
5 *Canary yellow (010)*
6 *Yellow ochre (032)*
7 *Grass green (220)*
8 *Peacock green (229)*
9 *True blue (161)*
10 *Ultramarine (140)*
11 *Indigo (159)*
12 *French grey 50% (405)*

REMEMBER
Each main colour is featured on its own page. The basic palette repeats once on every page.

MIXING SECONDARY COLOURS

The three primary colours, which are given this name because they can't be produced from mixtures of other colours, are red, yellow and blue. Pairs of these three colours, when mixed together, make the secondary colours – orange, green and purple. But it isn't quite as simple as this, because there are different versions of each of the primaries, and this affects the kind of mixture you make. The basic palette includes the two reds, yellows and blues shown on the simple colour wheel below; notice how different they appear when you see them side by side.

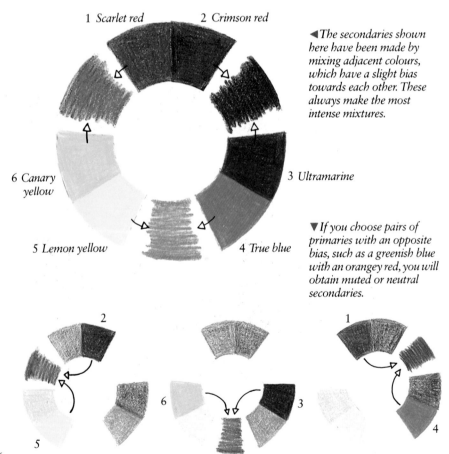

1 *Scarlet red*

2 *Crimson red*

◀*The secondaries shown here have been made by mixing adjacent colours, which have a slight bias towards each other. These always make the most intense mixtures.*

6 *Canary yellow*

3 *Ultramarine*

5 *Lemon yellow*

4 *True blue*

▼*If you choose pairs of primaries with an opposite bias, such as a greenish blue with an orangey red, you will obtain muted or neutral secondaries.*

OVERLAYING COLOURS

Striking differences in colour and tone can be achieved by overlaying the same two colours in different ways. Varying the pressure of the pencil point is an obvious way of affecting the depth of colour, but the end result can also be affected by the order in which the colours are laid. Although the top colour tends to be dominant, a light colour can still make an impact when covered by a darker one. The colours used below are deco yellow and imperial violet.

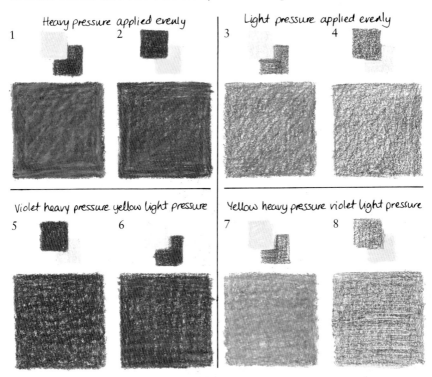

Top row *Laying the lighter colour heavily over the darker (1) has the effect of burnishing it (see page 8). The yellow laid below the purple (2) slightly modifies the darker colour. Yellow laid as the top colour (3) blends* *into the purple. It has a stronger effect when used first (4).*

***Bottom row** Here (5) the yellow is almost lost. The yellow laid on top of the purple (6) lightens and* *slightly changes it. The yellow is strong (7) but still blends with the purple. When the yellow is used first (8) the two colours "sit" separately.*

METHODS OF COLOUR MIXING

There are a variety of ways in which colours can be mixed on the paper. The one you choose will depend on the effect you want to achieve. For example, you may want a smooth transition from one colour to another or a thorough mixture of two or more colours. You may on the other hand prefer the livelier, more sparkling effect that comes from "optical mixing", where each of the colours used in the mixture can still be identified although the eye "reads" them as a third colour. It is worth experimenting with different methods, and some of the many possiblilities are shown below.

Open hatching strokes

Close hatching strokes

◀ *With hatching and crosshatching, linear marks are laid down side by side or across one another. You can build up tones as well as mixing colours "optically". The marks can be close together or left open, and the pencil point can vary.*

Even crosshatching

Varied crosshatching

◀ *Overlaying by shading produces a smoother blend, particularly if the colours are softened by rubbing with a tissue or rag. The pressure of the pencil point can be varied to fill the grain of the paper or leave areas of it visible.*

Colours shaded together

Shaded colours rubbed with tissue

Burnished with eraser

Burnished with white pencil

◀*Almost imperceptible blends can be created by burnishing. Colours are rubbed together and into the grain of the paper with a torchon (a rolled paper stump), a plastic eraser, or another coloured pencil making the surface smooth and slightly shiny.*

◀*In these examples, colours have been laid down dry and then washed over with water, causing them to mix. More dry colour can be laid on top if required with a brush or rag.*

Heavy blue over heavy red

Heavy red over heavy blue

Heavy blue over light red

Heavy red over light blue

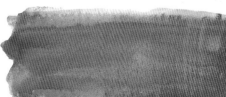

Graded blue to red

True blue – 161

Scarlet red	Process red	Blush	Lemon yellow
Canary yellow	Yellow ochre	Grass green	Peacock green
True blue	Ultramarine	Indigo blue	French grey 50%

070	090	071	240
010	032	220	229
161	140	159	405

Scarlet red	Process red	Blush	Lemon yellow
Canary yellow	Yellow ochre	Grass green	Peacock green
True blue	Ultramarine	Indigo blue	French grey 50%
070	090	071	240
010	032	220	229
161	140	159	405

Blue slate – 141

Scarlet red

Process red

Blush

Lemon yellow

Canary yellow

Yellow ochre

Grass green

Peacock green

True blue

Ultramarine

Indigo blue

French grey 50%

070

090

071

240

010

032

220

229

161

140

159

405

Scarlet red	Process red	Blush	Lemon yellow

Canary yellow	Yellow ochre	Grass green	Peacock green

True blue	Ultramarine	Indigo blue	French grey 50%

070	090	071	240

010	032	220	229

161	140	159	405

Imperial violet – 130

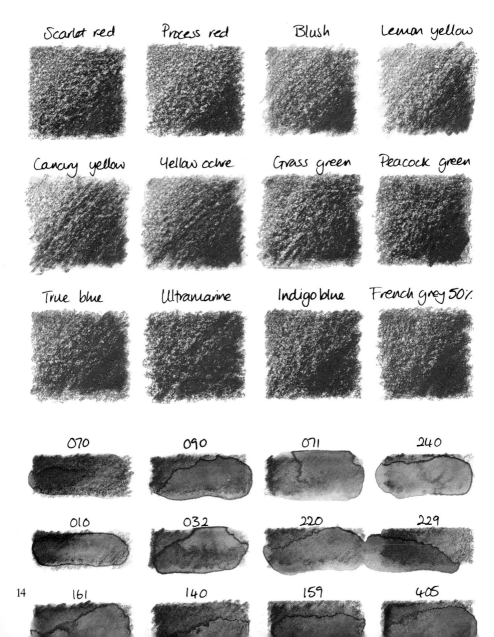

Scarlet red	Process red	Blush	Lemon yellow
Canary yellow	Yellow ochre	Grass green	Peacock green
True blue	Ultramarine	Indigo blue	French grey 50%

070	090	071	240
010	032	220	229
161	140	159	405

14

Indigo blue – 159

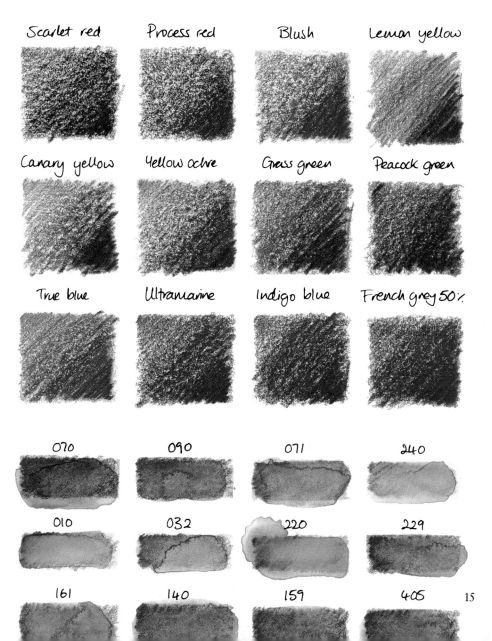

Scarlet red

Process red

Blush

Lemon yellow

Canary yellow

Yellow ochre

Grass green

Peacock green

True blue

Ultramarine

Indigo blue

French grey 50%

070

090

071

240

010

032

220

229

161

140

159

405

USING BLUES

Sue Lines – *Fishes*

14 × 11 ins

THE COLOUR EFFECTS in this lovely delicate drawing have been built up throughout by hatching and crosshatching. Using fine lines and sharp pencils, the artist has achieved very subtle graduations of tone and graceful modelling of form. The consistency of handling unifies the picture as well as providing an extra decorative dimension.

▶ *The form of the seaweed has been developed by altering the pressure of the pencil point and gently manipulating the direction of the strokes.*

▼ *The shadows on the body of the crab have been made by overlaying yellow ochre with various browns and blues. The blues and blue-greens echo the colours in the background, while the warm colours and touches of violet help to "lift" the crab from the ground.*

▲ *A lively surface effect is made by crosshatching over the systematic diagonal hatching of the background. Some areas are sufficiently dense to read as a continuous tone.*

◀ *The pinks used for the seaweed on the left are important in the composition, echoing the star and the paler pink on the top of the fish's body. All the pinks have been kept slightly "cool", to blend with the overall blue colour scheme.*

Peacock green – 229

Scarlet red

Process red

Blush

Lemon yellow

Canary yellow

Yellow ochre

Grass green

Peacock green

True blue

Ultramarine

Indigo blue

French grey 50%

070

090

071

240

010

032

220

229

161

140

159

405

Scarlet red

Process red

Blush

Lemon yellow

Canary yellow

Yellow ochre

Grass green

Peacock green

True blue

Ultramarine

Indigo blue

French grey 50%

070

090

071

240

010

032

220

229

161

140

159

405

True green – 201

Scarlet red

Process red

Blush

Lemon yellow

Canary yellow

Yellow ochre

Grass green

Peacock green

True blue

Ultramarine

Indigo blue

French grey 50%

070

090

071

240

010

032

220

229

161

140

159

405

Olive green – 225

Scarlet red	Process red	Blush	Lemon yellow
Canary yellow	Yellow ochre	Grass green	Peacock green
True blue	Ultramarine	Indigo blue	French grey 50%

070	090	071	240
010	032	220	229
161	140	159	405

21

Apple green – 221

Scarlet red

Process red

Blush

Lemon yellow

Canary yellow

Yellow ochre

Grass green

Peacock green

True blue

Ultramarine

Indigo blue

French grey 50%

070

090

071

240

010

032

220

229

22 161

140

159

405

Scarlet red	Process red	Blush	Lemon yellow
Canary yellow	Yellow ochre	Grass green	Peacock green
True blue	Ultramarine	Indigo blue	French grey 50%
070	090	071	240
010	032	220	229
161	140	159	405

23

Mixing greens

Deco yellow

Lemon yellow

Canary yellow

Yellow ochre

Sky blue   True blue   Ultramarine   Indigo blue

The pigment ratios for both sets of charts have been chosen to produce the best results.
For the equivalent colours in water-soluble pencil see Contents page.

Deco yellow

Lemon yellow

Canary yellow

Yellow ochre

Grass green   Peacock green   Olive green   Black

Using Greens

Jane Strother – *Muscadet Region*

8×6 ins approximately

THE FRESH SPRING atmosphere in this view of vineyards has been conveyed by using a unified palette of cool blues, violet and greens with some warm but light pinks and ochres. For the greens, true blue, blush and grass green were lightly shaded before more detailed drawing was done in stronger tones. Careful water washes blend colours and "knock back" shadows.

► *For the strong shadows under the eaves, violet washed with water has been laid over blush and yellow ochre. Pale orange pencil highlights the sunlit wall, and white areas are accentuated with gouache paint or diluted with a thin violet wash.*

▼ *The stones in the wall have been shaded with blush, yellow ochre and olive green. The shadows are drawn in indigo and peacock green, and the whole area softened with a light wash.*

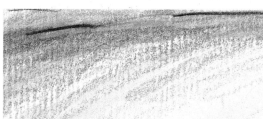

▲ *Loose drawing follows the form of the road, giving movement to the foreground. The broad, grainy marks made in yellow ochre, deco yellow and olive green are blended with water. Heavier pressure with a blue-violet pencil has been used for the shadow.*

◄ *Peacock green, indigo and grass green describe the form of the tree. Flecks of the underlying blush show through the foliage, creating a link between the tree and the receding fields.*

◀The purple shadows recede quite dramatically and the green stripes "come forward", thus achieving the effect of a vineyard by the use of colour alone. Blush has been used beneath these colours, unifying this area with the rest of the landscape.

Lemon yellow – 240

Scarlet red	Process red	Blush	Lemon yellow

Canary yellow	Yellow ochre	Grass green	Peacock green

True blue	Ultramarine	Indigo blue	French grey 50%

070	090	071	240

010	032	220	229

161	140	159	405

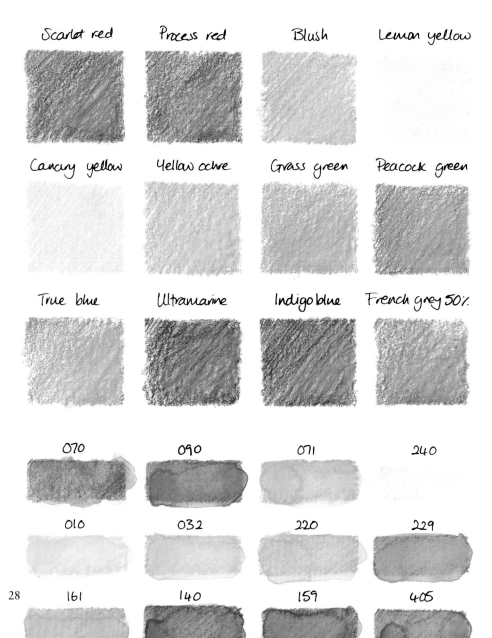

Canary yellow – 010

| Scarlet red | Process red | Blush | Lemon yellow |

| Canary yellow | Yellow ochre | Grass green | Peacock green |

| True blue | Ultramarine | Indigo blue | French grey 50% |

| 070 | 090 | 071 | 240 |

| 010 | 032 | 220 | 229 |

| 161 | 140 | 159 | 405 |

Scarlet red

Process red

Blush

Lemon yellow

Canary yellow

Yellow ochre

Grass green

Peacock green

True blue

Ultramarine

Indigo blue

French grey 50%

070

090

071

240

010

032

220

229

161

140

159

405

Yellow ochre – 032

Scarlet red

Process red

Blush

Lemon yellow

Canary yellow

Yellow ochre

Grass green

Peacock green

True blue

Ultramarine

Indigo blue

French grey 50%

070

090

071

240

010

032

220

229

161

140

159

405

Golden rod – 035

Scarlet red　Process red　Blush　Lemon yellow

Canary yellow　Yellow ochre　Grass green　Peacock green

True blue　Ultramarine　Indigo blue　French grey 50%

070　090　071　240

010　032　220　229

　161　140　159　405

Pumpkin orange – 062

| Scarlet red | Process red | Blush | Lemon yellow |

| Canary yellow | Yellow ochre | Grass green | Peacock green |

| True blue | Ultramarine | Indigo blue | French grey 50% |

| 070 | 090 | 071 | 240 |

| 010 | 032 | 220 | 229 |

| 161 | 140 | 159 | 405 |

33

Mixing oranges

Deco yellow

Lemon yellow

Canary yellow

Yellow ochre

34

Salmon pink   Pumpkin orange   Pink   Scarlet red

The pigment ratios for both sets of charts have been chosen to produce the best results.
For the equivalent colours in water-soluble pencil see Contents page.

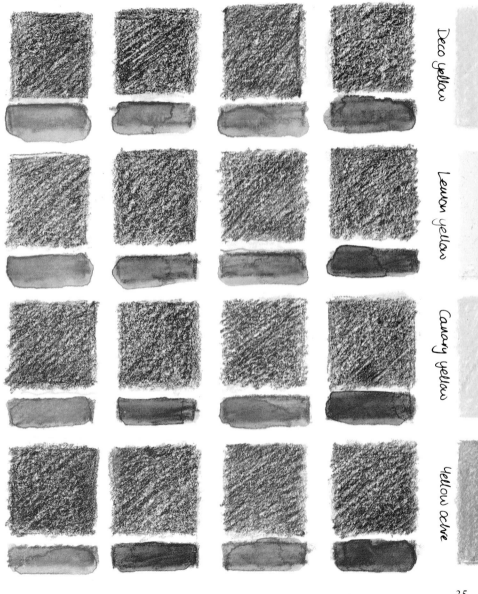

Deco yellow

Lemon yellow

Canary yellow

Yellow ochre

Process red   Crimson red   Terracotta   Raspberry

USING BRIGHT COLOURS

Jane Hughes – *Pinboard*

23 × 16¼ ins

IN THIS DETAILED drawing of a cluttered pinboard the artist has used a large palette of colours straight from the box, with colour mixing kept to a minimum. Where a range of vivid colours is required it is not always practical to rely on mixing, which typically provides more subtle effects. Various methods have been employed to build up different textures and surfaces, from the subtle shading used for the transparent wrapper to the dense, flat areas of colour which represent opaque printed colour.

◀ *The dominant colour in this part of the picture is noticeably red, with several different hues used. Shadows are created with darker reds, with touches of blue and brown. The light, fluffy texture of the feather has been wonderfully captured with sensitive manipulation of the pencil.*

▶ *The highlights on the transparent wrapper have been created by using an eraser, a method which is only really successful on lightly pencilled areas. The careful shading on this, the most three-dimensional object in the picture, contrasts with the flatly applied colour elsewhere.*

Salmon pink – 051

Scarlet red

Process red

Blush

Lemon yellow

Canary yellow

Yellow ochre

Grass green

Peacock green

True blue

Ultramarine

Indigo blue

French grey 50%

070

090

071

240

010

032

220

229

161

140

159

405

Blush – 071

Scarlet red

Process red

Blush

Lemon yellow

Canary yellow

Yellow ochre

Grass green

Peacock green

True blue

Ultramarine

Indigo blue

French grey 50%

070

090

071

240

010

032

220

229

161

140

159

405

39

Rosy beige – 403

Scarlet red

Process red

Blush

Lemon yellow

Canary yellow

Yellow ochre

Grass green

Peacock green

True blue

Ultramarine

Indigo blue

French grey 50%

070

090

071

240

010

032

220

229

161

140

159

405

Scarlet red

Process red

Blush

Lemon yellow

Canary yellow

Yellow ochre

Grass green

Peacock green

True blue

Ultramarine

Indigo blue

French grey 50%

070

090

071

240

010

032

220

229

161

140

159

405

Crimson red – 080

Scarlet red

Process red

Blush

Lemon yellow

Canary yellow

Yellow ochre

Grass green

Peacock green

True blue

Ultramarine

Indigo blue

French grey 50%

070

090

071

240

010

032

220

229

42   161

140

159

405

Scarlet red	Process red	Blush	Lemon yellow
Canary yellow	Yellow ochre	Grass green	Peacock green
True blue	Ultramarine	Indigo blue	French grey 50%

070	090	071	240
010	032	220	229
161	140	159	405

43

Raspberry – 085

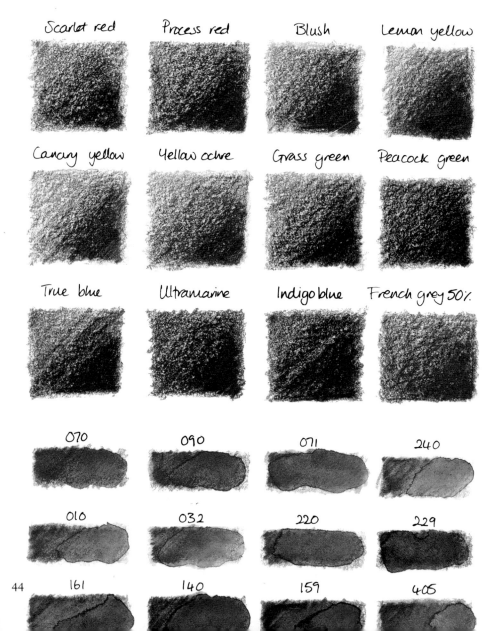

| Scarlet red | Process red | Blush | Lemon yellow |

| Canary yellow | Yellow ochre | Grass green | Peacock green |

| True blue | Ultramarine | Indigo blue | French grey 50% |

| 070 | 090 | 071 | 240 |

| 010 | 032 | 220 | 229 |

| 161 | 140 | 159 | 405 |

Process red – 090

Scarlet red

Process red

Blush

Lemon yellow

Canary yellow

Yellow ochre

Grass green

Peacock green

True blue

Ultramarine

Indigo blue

French grey 50%

070

090

071

240

010

032

220

229

161

140

159

405

Light violet – 111

Scarlet red	Process red	Blush	Lemon yellow

Canary yellow	Yellow ochre	Grass green	Peacock green

True blue	Ultramarine	Indigo blue	French grey 50%

070	090	071	240

010	032	220	229

161	140	159	405

Scarlet red

Process red

Blush

Lemon yellow

Canary yellow

Yellow ochre

Grass green

Peacock green

True blue

Ultramarine

Indigo blue

French grey 50%

070

090

071

240

010

032

220

229

161

140

159

405

Mixing purples

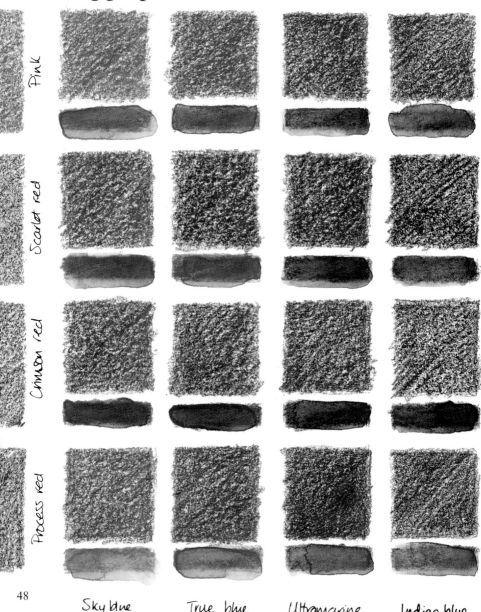

Pink

Scarlet red

Crimson red

Process red

Sky blue

True blue

Ultramarine

Indigo blue

The pigment ratios for both sets of charts have been chosen to produce the best results. For the equivalent colours in water-soluble pencil see Contents page.

Pink

Scarlet red

Crimson red

Process red

Blue slate   Light violet   Violet   Imperial violet

OPTICAL MIXING

Carl Melegari – *Street Walking*

20 × 15 ins

WHEN TWO COLOURS which are close in tone are laid down next to each other they merge in the eye and read as one colour. The artist has made exciting use of this principle, building up wonderfully vivid and shimmering colours with close diagonal strokes. This vigorous use of the pencils, together with the free, flowing outlines of the figures, gives an excellent impression of movement.

▶ *The darkest colours have been achieved by the addition of black, but several other colours have been used beneath and allowed to show through. Viewed on its own, this detail of the picture looks like nothing more than a set of strips; optical mixing relies on the context as well as a degree of distance.*

◀ *It is fascinating to see the number of colours used here. Although the eye reads the figure as red, there are blues, blue-greens and yellows as well as reds, violets and pinks.*

51

Burnt umber – 409

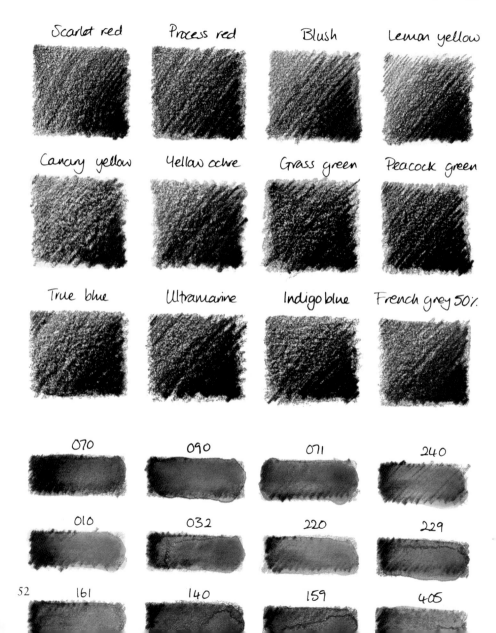

Scarlet red

Process red

Blush

Lemon yellow

Canary yellow

Yellow ochre

Grass green

Peacock green

True blue

Ultramarine

Indigo blue

French grey 50%

070

090

071

240

010

032

220

229

52

161

140

159

405

Sienna brown – 059

Scarlet red

Process red

Blush

Lemon yellow

Canary yellow

Yellow ochre

Grass green

Peacock green

True blue

Ultramarine

Indigo blue

French grey 50%

070

090

071

240

010

032

220

229

161

140

159

405

Terracotta – 065

Scarlet red

Process red

Blush

Lemon yellow

Canary yellow

Yellow ochre

Grass green

Peacock green

True blue

Ultramarine

Indigo blue

French grey 50%

070

090

071

240

010

032

220

229

161

140

159

405

Bronze – 025

Scarlet red | Process red | Blush | Lemon yellow

Canary yellow | Yellow ochre | Grass green | Peacock green

True blue | Ultramarine | Indigo blue | French grey 50%

070 | 090 | 071 | 240

010 | 032 | 220 | 229

161 | 140 | 159 | 405

55

Mixing browns: two colours

The pigment ratios for both sets of charts have been chosen to produce the best results.

Pumpkin orange

Scarlet red

Raspberry

Crimson red

Ultramarine   Burnt umber   Grass green   Black

Mixing browns: three colours

For the equivalent colours in water-soluble pencil see Contents page.

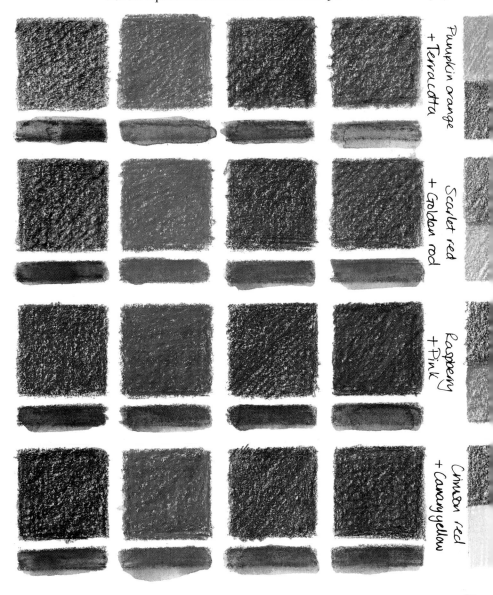

Pumpkin orange + Terracotta

Scarlet red + Golden rod

Raspberry + Pink

Crimson red + Canary yellow

Indigo blue   French grey 50%   Violet   Olive green

57

USING DARK COLOURS

Phil Wildman – *Backstreet Football*

23 × 33 ins approximately

ALTHOUGH THE COLOURS are all relatively dark they are far from sombre, and the eye is drawn immediately to the rich red-brown of the sunlit wall and the vivid blue of the sky. The wall is the focal point of the picture, and is more "worked-up" than other areas. The foreground, although well observed, remains sketchy, allowing the eye to pass over and above it to the buildings themselves.

◀ *The end wall is in deep shadow, and the pencil has been built up thickly, with overlays of blue, brown and black very slightly graded towards the bottom. Here again the blind impressing method has been used to describe the slant of the roof tiles, and the directional strokes used for the sky give an attractive sense of movement.*

▼ *The browns and rusts in this area are dense and vibrant, complemented by the deep, dark blue of the roof. The shadow of the chimney, an important part of the composition, has been created by laying a darker brown over the rich rust colour.*

◄In some areas of the picture the artist has used a method called blind impressing, in which lines are made by drawing or scribbling on the paper with a point. These remain white when shaded over. Here the technique has allowed him to suggest the texture of the wall.

French grey 50% – 405

Scarlet red | Process red | Blush | Lemon yellow

Canary yellow | Yellow ochre | Grass green | Peacock green

True blue | Ultramarine | Indigo blue | French grey 50%

070 | 090 | 071 | 240

010 | 032 | 220 | 229

161 | 140 | 159 | 405

Cool grey 50% – 005

Scarlet red	Process red	Blush	Lemon yellow

Canary yellow	Yellow ochre	Grass green	Peacock green

True blue	Ultramarine	Indigo blue	French grey 50%

070	090	071	240

010	032	220	229

161	140	159	405

 # Black – 009

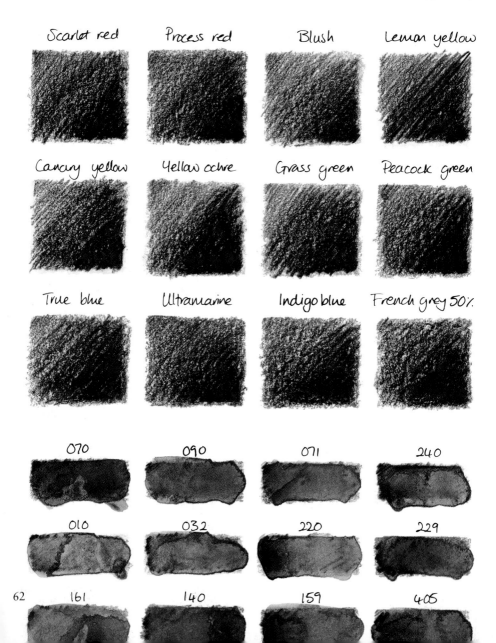

Scarlet red | Process red | Blush | Lemon yellow

Canary yellow | Yellow ochre | Grass green | Peacock green

True blue | Ultramarine | Indigo blue | French grey 50%

070 | 090 | 071 | 240

010 | 032 | 220 | 229

161 | 140 | 159 | 405

Scarlet red

Process red

Blush

Lemon yellow

Canary yellow

Yellow ochre

Grass green

Peacock green

True blue

Ultramarine

Indigo blue

French grey 50%

070

090

071

240

010

032

220

229

161

140

159

405

CREDITS

CONTRIBUTING ARTISTS
16 Sue Lines; **26** Jane Strother; **36** Jane Hughes;
50 Carl Melegari; **58** Phil Wildman

Senior Editor
Hazel Harrison

Art Director
Moira Clinch

Designer
Clare Baggaley

Typeset by West End Studios, Eastbourne
Manufactured by Bright Arts (Singapore) Pte. Ltd.
Printed in Singapore by Tien Wah

The publishers would like to thank
Berol and Caran d'Ache for kindly supplying
the materials for this book